Original title:
Spider Plants and Solace

Copyright © 2025 Creative Arts Management OÜ
All rights reserved.

Author: Isaac Ravenscroft
ISBN HARDBACK: 978-1-80581-753-6
ISBN PAPERBACK: 978-1-80581-280-7
ISBN EBOOK: 978-1-80581-753-6

Touching the Heart of Nature

In a pot, they wiggle with glee,
Tiny tendrils, wild and free.
They dance through dust with a flair,
Secretly plotting world takeover despair.

With friends in green, they chat all day,
"Let's grow taller, what do you say?"
They whisper jokes in the morning sun,
Swapping tales of gardening fun.

Leafy Lightness

Leaves are flopping, roots are twirling,
In our home, the green is swirling.
Caught in laughter, full of cheer,
Who knew plants could be so dear?

They stretch their arms to reach the light,
Showing off their leafy might.
A jungle party, come take a seat,
Each leaf sways to a rhythm sweet.

Glistening in the Light

Under the sun, they shimmer bright,
Green acrobats, what a sight!
Photosynthesis – their favorite game,
For a snack, they're never the same!

With little pots, they sing their song,
"Join us, friend, you can't go wrong!"
A leafy laugh, they sway and spin,
In their kingdom, you're bound to win.

A Refuge in Growth

In corners where sunshine beams,
They plot their leafy little dreams.
'Water me!' they gently tease,
Dancing to nature's sweet breeze.

They hold the secrets of the earth,
In their dance, we find rebirth.
With spiky jokes and leafy grins,
Every day, adventure begins.

Whispers of Green in the Quiet Room

In a corner, they sway with ease,
Little friends dancing in a breeze.
They wiggle and giggle without a care,
Pretending they're on a sunlit fair.

A sip of water makes them cheer,
They've got the best life, oh dear!
With every leaf, they strike a pose,
A photo op, goodness knows!

Threads of Calm Beneath the Sun

Whispering secrets, oh so sly,
Beneath the rays, they seem to fly.
Stretching their arms, they welcome light,
Chasing away shadows, causing delight.

In this sunny nook, they play hide and seek,
Their leafy laughs reach a tiny peak.
With every rustle, a ticklish tone,
They're the sweetest jesters, never alone.

Lush Foliage and Gentle Dreams

Bouncing back from a lazy noon,
Leaves reminisce to their own tune.
Tickled by the wind, they sway and leap,
Crafting stories, oh so deep.

In their green realm, laughter flows,
Like gossiping friends, everyone knows.
As the sun dips, they cozy up tight,
Dreaming of mischief, until the night.

A Tapestry of Leaves and Light

Each leaf hangs like a quirky smile,
A tapestry woven with playful style.
Spinning tales of joy and cheer,
In their leafy kingdom, all's sincere.

They've got the rhythm, they set the tone,
A sway of verdure, they're never alone.
In jolly colors, they bask and beam,
Dancing in daylight, living the dream.

Nature's Gentle Embrace

In a pot on my shelf, they dance with glee,
With leaves like arms, they reach for me.
They wiggle and wobble, a funny sight,
As if they're doing yoga, morning light.

Droplets of water, they joyfully sip,
I swear I heard one say, "Take a dip!"
A green parade, oh what a scene,
Chatting away, like leaves in a dream.

Lush Comforts of Home

These leafy buddies, oh what a crew,
They make me laugh until I'm blue.
With each new shoot, they start to tease,
"More sun, more fun! We're a leafy breeze!"

Hanging down like a funky hat,
In the corner, they wiggle and chat.
I hear them giggle, oh what a jest,
"Life's too short, just grow and rest!"

Serenity in Leaves

In cozy corners they sway and sway,
Like tiny dancers leading the ballet.
With roots deep down and leaves so bright,
They whisper secrets all through the night.

They often claim that they are wise,
"Life's tough, take root; just watch the skies!"
In their gentle sway, humor unfolds,
Nature's laughter, a joy that holds.

The Quiet Growth

Here they grow, without a care,
Looking so cute with leafy flair.
They plot in silence, their leafy dreams,
"More light, more laughs, or so it seems!"

They peek from pots with a cheeky grin,
Encouraging me to join in the spin.
In the stillness, a chuckle is found,
In green companions, joy knows no bounds.

Nature's Reassurance

In a pot, a dancer sways,
With leaves that laugh and play.
Chasing dust with playful flair,
Who knew plants could have such hair?

Lurking corners, they conspire,
To catch your thoughts and lift them higher.
Their whispers tickle, oh so sweet,
As green companions sway and meet.

They wrangle sunlight, stretch with glee,
In every home, they want to be.
Living comics, roots so spry,
With every glance, they wink and sigh.

Beneath the windows, their feet take hold,
In a silent chatter, their tales unfold.
Nature's buddies in the afternoon light,
Bringing chuckles, oh what a sight!

A Calm Canopy

Under green, the world feels weird,
Those leafy limbs have got us cheered.
Hanging out like nature's crew,
They offer comfort, just for you.

In the shade, stories unfold,
Of botanical dreams, brave and bold.
A chat with leaves, don't be shy—
They'll tickle your mind and make you fly.

Roots reaching out, on a quest,
To find the sun and be their best.
Stretching limbs like they've found a throne,
In their green realm, you're never alone.

Life's worries drift under their embrace,
With laughter caught in every space.
A canopy that sways with cheer,
So come, my friend, rest over here.

Growing Stillness

In a pot of leafy dreams,
A world of fun, or so it seems.
Poking through the soil so deep,
They laugh aloud while you just sleep.

Cheeky roots in a digging race,
With every new leaf, they find their place.
A silent giggle with every sprout,
In the house, they twist and shout.

With every sip of water shared,
Their gleeful dance says: 'We've prepared!'
Like tiny jesters dressed in green,
Bringing joy yet to be seen.

While you ponder and feel thrice,
They weave their magic, oh how nice!
A chuckle here, a wink or two,
In this calm space, they smile for you.

Bathed in Green Light

In the glow of morning's rays,
The leaves emit their silly plays.
A jungle gym for dust and air,
Whispers of joy hang everywhere.

They celebrate the sun's warm kiss,
In a dance that feels like pure bliss.
With every shadow, tales unfold,
In this green glow, we're never old.

Bouncing leaves, a giggling crew,
Plotting mischief, oh what a view!
In their realm of twirls and sways,
Even shadows can't help but blaze.

So join the fun, take a seat,
Gather 'round for this leafy treat.
In the garden, laughter's bright,
Bathed in green, it feels so right!

A Symphony of Green and Stillness

In corners where the shadows play,
A friendly leaf begins to sway,
It giggles light as breezes blow,
Pretending it's a plant on show.

With tendrils offering playful hugs,
They wave at me, like little bugs,
A dance of chlorophyll and cheer,
A green retreat from daily fear.

Beneath the sun, they stretch and yawn,
"Don't you wish that you were drawn,
To sip the sun and sip some tea?"
Their antics bring such joy to me.

When folks declare, 'Oh, what a chore!'
These leafy pals say, "Give us more!'
With every water drop, they prance,
A thriving foliage, in their dance.

Lush Reveries in Secluded Nooks

In quiet spaces, they reside,
A jungle where my worries hide,
Amidst the clutter, there's a grin,
As vibrant greens bring joy within.

Each pot a kingdom, each leaf a throne,
They jest, 'You're never all alone!'
With every sip of morning dew,
They wink and nod just like a crew.

When co-workers sigh of deadlines tight,
I smile and say, "It'll be alright,"
For in their rustling, I can hear,
A symphony of laughter, clear.

A gentle breeze through windows wide,
They sway, suggest, "Enjoy the ride!"
As pots parade on tabletops,
Their leafy jokes never stop.

Heartfelt Green in Familiar Spaces

In every nook where sunlight gleams,
They weave their vines, fulfill my dreams,
With every twist, a tale unfolds,
Of verdant ventures and leafy holds.

Their whispers carry, light and free,
"Hey, friend, come share some tea with me!"
In gathered friends or solo chats,
They join the fun, embellishing spats.

When I forget to give a drink,
They thrive, and without fuss, they wink,
Their silent protest, oh so sly,
"You'll regret it—so don't deny!"

As I walk past, I hear them tease,
"Come join the party, plant with ease!"
With every leaf, a quirky jest,
In cozy corners, they are blessed.

Growing Tranquility in Urban Life

Amidst the rush of city sights,
These leafy beings spark delight,
With roots that grip the pot so snug,
They contemplate a lilting hug.

In crowded rooms, they host their dreams,
Inventing joys, or so it seems,
Their leafy laughter fills the air,
"Don't stress, relax – just stop and stare."

With sunlight leaking through the pane,
They dance as if they know no pain,
"Let's throw a party, gather round,"
In nature's whimsy, joy is found.

As pigeons coo and motors hum,
They stay in joy while chaos drums,
A quirky crew, so green and bright,
In urban jungles, they ignite.

Nature's Blanket

A pot of green sits with flair,
Tiny fingers reach for air.
Hiding dust in a leafy hug,
Whispering secrets just like a bug.

On shelves they prance, in sun's embrace,
Twirling softly, full of grace.
Do they plot for a dance in night?
Or giggle quietly, full of delight?

With each new sprout, a cheeky grin,
A green parade that won't give in.
Who needs a circus for some fun?
When leaf acrobatics just begun?

In this cozy jungle, no need for shoes,
Just laughter and leaves, and some funky moves.
The soil lends cheer, it's quite a treat,
Nature's blanket, oh so sweet!

Dance of the Drift

Roots wiggling like they're on display,
In life's grand show, they steal the sway.
Who knew stillness could be this bold?
With each sway, a tale unfolds.

They're queens of calm in their leafy attire,
Searching for sunshine, their one true desire.
A gentle bob here, a twirl so grand,
Leaves like dancers, hand in hand.

Pot buddies cuddled, a cozy bunch,
Sip water on a Sunday brunch.
A leaf floats down, like a clumsy break,
Landing softly, with a giggle, "Oops, my mistake!"

As daylight wanes, the party's a balm,
Though rooted, they dance, so carefree and calm.
Room's alive, with smiles all around,
In the drift, joy knows no bound.

Swaying to a Silent Song

In corners where shadows play,
Leaves sway gently, come what may.
With no music, they find their beat,
Their rhythm soft, a leafy greet.

Each morning bright, they wake and yawn,
Stirring with glee at the break of dawn.
Oh to be green, a carefree sprite,
Dancing alone, a delightful sight!

A breeze whispers tales from afar,
Each leaf a dancer, a shining star.
No feet to tap but still they groove,
In this quiet space, they smoothly move.

With every shake and joyful sway,
They paint the air, come join their play.
A silent tune, a giggling throng,
In harmony, they can't go wrong.

In the Company of Leaves

Gather 'round, my greenish friends,
With laughter that never ends.
In this leafy camp, let's unwind,
Sharing tales of the curious kind.

One leaf claimed it saw a bug,
Another said, "No, that's a shrug!"
They poke and prod with all their might,
In this company, all feels right.

Swirling in shadows, banter flows,
Life's highs and lows, everyone knows.
They giggle and chat as they swing,
The sound of joy is what they bring.

In this room, laughter fills the air,
A cozy nook, rich with care.
With leafy grins and stories grand,
In the company of leaves, you'll always stand!

Nurtured Spirits

In the corner sits a green delight,
With twisted leaves that dance in light.
A guardian of peace, no need for a crown,
It waves hello without a frown.

As I water it, I sip my tea,
Its gentle sway makes me feel free.
It knows the secret of joy so pure,
In its green embrace, I feel secure.

Whenever I'm down, it gives a grin,
A little therapy from within.
Who knew a plant could bring such cheer?
I laugh at my worries when it's near.

With every leaf, it shouts, "Let's play!"
"Grow a little wild, it's a plants' buffet!"
So here's to the joy, the leafy delight,
Together we bloom, making life bright.

The Art of Letting Go

A pot of green that takes the stage,
In a world of chaos, it's all the rage.
With a little sunlight and a dash of fun,
It reminds me that we all can run.

Each leaf a laugh, each root a joke,
Who knew joy bloomed from such humble smoke?
I trim and snip, set worries adrift,
And find that my heart starts to lift.

"Let go!" it whispers, "Don't hold so tight,
Life's a dance, it's meant to be light."
I giggle as it stretches wide,
Teaching me how to take life in stride.

So here's to the green, the giggly vibe,
The plant and I make quite the tribe.
In the art of letting go, we find,
A world of laughter, both gentle and kind.

Whispers from the Windowsill

Perched on the sill, all prim and neat,
It watches the world with roots at its feet.
"Hey there, friend, why the long face?"
"Let's rock this day with a little grace!"

A breeze wanders in, tickles the leaves,
"It's time for fun, so roll up your sleeves!"
Together we plot mischievous schemes,
Turning kitchen chaos into our dreams.

With every droplet that drips from the can,
It shares the wisdom of the plant clan.
"Life's a circus, don't take a bow,
Just twirl and giggle, live in the now!"

So here I sit with my leafy muse,
Crafting little moments, no need to refuse.
Whispers from green help laugh my way,
Elevating the mundane to a happy play.

Green Guardians of Calm

In a pot of mischief, life begins,
With leafy guardians and their goofy grins.
They sway to the music of the afternoon sun,
Cheering me on, "Hey, let's have fun!"

A snip here and there, a little snack too,
Their leafy laughter, I can't get enough of you.
They soak up my worries, a detox spree,
Turning my frown into glee, whee!

Every sprout a silly dance, every stem a cheer,
Helping to lighten my heaviest fears.
"Join us," they echo, "and shake with delight,
We'll keep your spirits on this happy flight!"

So here's to my greens, my merry brigade,
Creating calm in their unique charade.
With joyful antics and vibes that don't tire,
They guardian my heart with leafy desire.

Leafy Guardians of the Heart

In a pot they sit, looking so sly,
With leaves like fingers, reaching for the sky.
They eavesdrop on secrets, like good friends do,
Whispering soft giggles when the day is blue.

Petals of green, they dance with delight,
In the morning sun, they put up a fight.
Chasing away worries with their leafy charm,
Who knew a plant could keep you warm?

They spin tales of nature, full of jest,
In their leafy laughter, we find our rest.
With a wink and a bob, they sway to the beat,
Guardians of happiness, oh, aren't they sweet?

So here's to the greens, with their playful tunes,
In the quiet of home, they help chase the moons.
Plant pals for life, with smiles to impart,
Leafy guardians here, they heal the heart.

Tranquil Spirals in the Swaying Breeze

In the cool of the shade, they catch some air,
Spiraling leaves that twirl without care.
A merry little jig in the gentle light,
Bringing chuckles and giggles, oh what a sight!

With their little pixie ways, they sway on a whim,
Dancing like children on a sunbeam's rim.
Who knew that greens could spark such delight?
Sprouting up joy, like a plant-themed kite!

They whisper sweet nothings, soft as a dream,
Bathtubs of laughter in their leafy regime.
A party of greens, with no need for a name,
Spirals of joy, playing a happy game.

So dance with the leaves in your cozy space,
Let nature's fine humor draw a smile on your face.
In joyful tunes sung by each leafy friend,
Laughter and peace that never will end.

The Gentle Caress of Nature's Hand

Oh, the gentle caress of the soft, leafy scene,
With vines that hug tightly and air so serene.
They giggle below, with a rustle and sway,
Tickling our hearts in their charming display.

Little green whispers floating around,
With a wink and a smile, your troubles are drowned.
In the light, they shimmer like comedy's grace,
Oh, what a delight, this leafy embrace!

They tell silly tales of the soil below,
While sprouting up laughter like seeds in a row.
A garden of joy, as they lean on me,
These green little jesters, as happy as can be.

So welcome the comforts, don't shy from their cheer,
They'll dance you through moments, and always draw near.
With playful green fingers, they flourish and play,
Turning gray days into sunshine, come what may.

Serenity Grows in Tender Greens

In corners and nooks, where laughter does bloom,
Tiny green warriors, embracing the room.
With each tender leaf, they weave a bright scheme,
Whisking away worries, like a swift little dream.

They nod when we chat, like they know all the lore,
With roots intertwined, they ask us for more.
Bringing soft chuckles on days that feel tough,
The comfort they grant is more than enough.

So sit with your greens, and share all the tales,
Of mischievous dreams, where laughter prevails.
In their leafy embrace, all trouble seems small,
A home filled with giggles is the best place of all.

So raise up a toast to their glorious hue,
A tribute to greens that see us on through.
For in every soft leaf, a chuckle is seen,
Oh, how sweet is the joy in the tender, bright green!

Soft Textures of Nature

In the corner, leaves are bold,
Bouncing back, they never fold.
Whispers tickle, just for fun,
Nature's laughter, second to none.

Pots are scattered, chaos reigns,
Greenery dances, ignoring chains.
Socks and shoes in disarray,
Blame the plants for leading astray.

A spider lurks in leafy guise,
Does it weave, or just despise?
Giggling, flicking, tendrils sway,
Who knew that leaves could play all day?

Blooming mishaps, like a joke,
Roots entangled, life's a poke.
Nature's ticklish, light and free,
In this green room, you'll laugh with glee.

Sanctuary of Quietness

In stillness, they stretch and yawn,
Pretending they're a morning dawn.
Silence wrapped in leafy frames,
Who knew calmness played such games?

Sipping sunbeams, sipping fate,
Branches jive, it's quite a state.
Visitors come to take a peek,
'They're just plants,' someone will speak.

Potted friends with quirky quirks,
Show off leaves like silly perks.
Whispers of laughter fill the air,
Calmness finds a way to share.

Nature's humor, soft and bright,
Serenity has no fright.
In a corner, view the scene,
Where joy grows wild, lush, and green.

Timeless in Foliage

In ancient pots, they sway around,
Not a care, they're tightly bound.
Casting shadows, always keen,
Roots and tales, like evergreen.

Green-armed jokers in the room,
Playing tricks, they thrive on bloom.
Tickling sunlight, bending low,
With every breeze, they steal the show.

Each leaf a smile, a playful wink,
Nature's jesters make you think.
When life's heavy, just come near,
These green pals chase away the fear.

Ageless stories spun with cheer,
Whispered secrets rooted here.
With every twist and leafy dance,
They invite you to take a chance.

Reflections in Green

Mirrored leaves in watery dreams,
Where sunlight glints and laughter seems.
A leafy duo at the bay,
Nature's giggles, bright and gay.

Waving fronds like silly hands,
Growing loud in quiet lands.
Reflective smiles from every seam,
A garden plot feels like a dream.

Look closely, humor's all about,
In every leaf, there's joy throughout.
A dance of breezes, whispers fun,
Nature's laughter, never done.

The world's a stage, and they perform,
In gentle style, they break the norm.
To find comfort, just lean in,
Green reflections make you grin.

Sanctuary Amongst the Silent Stalks

In corners green with gentle sway,
A leafy friend who loves to play.
With roots that dance, they twist and twine,
They whisper jokes, quite benign.

In sunlight's glow, they take a bow,
While we sit back and furrow a brow.
These leafy clowns, they grow and cheer,
A comedy show, oh dear, oh dear!

They droop a bit, then perk right up,
Like socialites with fancy cups.
With every leaf that jumps in glee,
A giggle springs from every tree.

So here's to greens that make us laugh,
Their vibrant tales, a happy craft.
Amongst the stalks, we find our way,
To joy that sprouts, day after day.

Botanical Refuge of the Soul

In jungle realms of potted grace,
Nature's jesters, in this place.
They catch the dust, they sip the light,
Turning woes to sheer delight.

With long green arms that reach and wave,
They coax us on, so bold and brave.
In leafy laughter, stress departs,
These playful greens steal anxious hearts.

The way they hang, a funny sight,
Looking like they're ready to fight!
But with their charm, they're all disarmed,
In laughter's arms, we're all charmed.

So let's embrace this leafy crew,
In every shade of vibrant hue.
With every giggle, life feels bright,
In their refuge, we take flight.

Healing Touch of Nature's Tongues

With fronds that flutter, like they talk,
In quiet corners, they quietly squawk.
They beam with joys that branch and climb,
Tickling woes with leafy rhyme.

They stretch their leaves, giving a grin,
Inviting us to join their spin.
Their gentle sway makes worries flee,
In foliage found, we feel so free.

Oh, the pot that holds such zest,
A green comedian on a quest.
They tease the air with vibrant flair,
A funny friend who's always there.

So take a seat beside their cheer,
With every glance, you'll crack a sneer.
In nature's quirk, our hearts take wing,
Amongst their tongues, we dance and sing.

Peaceful Knots in Foliage's Hold

In leafy knots, our laughter grows,
With every twist, a new tale flows.
They smile so wide, with sunshine beams,
These leafy pals fulfill our dreams.

With braided grace, they sway and tease,
Looping low to breeze with ease.
A natural jest, they juggle light,
In their embrace, the world feels right.

So gather round, let's share a laugh,
With potted friends, on joy's behalf.
Their nature's dance makes spirits soar,
In peaceful knots, we demand more!

So here we stand, with smiles bright,
Amongst these greens, pure delight.
In cheerful company, we blend,
Forever grateful for this trend.

Foliage and Stillness

Leaves dance lightly in the breeze,
They giggle at the buzzing bees.
Roots set deep in warm, bright earth,
Claiming space with quirky mirth.

Sunbeams tickle every shade,
Whispers of a light brigade.
A garden trickster's grand parade,
Nature's jester, unafraid.

Planters sway on dancing feet,
With secrets brewing, oh so sweet.
They plot their stunts, both sly and neat,
In green attire, they feel elite.

So come and join this leafy spree,
With plants that laugh, your heart is free.
A symphony of leaves and glee,
In every nook, a jubilee.

Nature's Soft Tapestry

Fabric stitched with leafy care,
Threads of laughter fill the air.
Spines that arch and twist with flair,
Let's weave a tale without a scare.

Pots are grinning, full of cheer,
Each leaf a smile, crystal clear.
Nature's humor draws us near,
In verdant realms, we lose our fear.

A dance of roots beneath our feet,
Comedic dates in earthy suite.
Hilarity in every beat,
Where plants and giggles meet and greet.

So gather 'round, bring tinsel style,
Let nature's charm make you smile.
Beneath its cloak, we can compile,
A yarn of fun that stretches a mile.

Chasing Sunbeams

Along the sill, they stretch and strut,
With happy leaves, they show their guts.
Poking out to chase the light,
In a dance of sheer delight.

Sipping rays, with cups held high,
Whispering secrets to the sky.
Reaching high, they flirt with fate,
Giving shade, but feeling great.

One wiggles left, the other sways,
The sun provides their jolly phase.
With every beam, they jest and play,
A leafy comedy display.

So let the sunbeams weave their fun,
In every leaf, a laughing pun.
Unplug your woes, and on the run,
Dance with the greens, 'til day is done.

Tranquil Vines

Vines waltz sweetly, twist and twine,
In leafy laughter, they align.
Whispering secrets, soft and sly,
Winks exchanged as time floats by.

A vine's ambition? Climb so high,
To reach the clouds, oh my, oh my!
With every inch, they boast, they sigh,
Like nature's pranksters in the sky.

Gently wrapping 'round each post,
Nature's clingy, playful ghost.
With swirling grace, they love to coast,
In green embrace, they brag the most.

So join this vine-filled comedy,
With laughter shared, the wild and free.
In nature's arms, we'll always be,
A twist of joy, a jubilee.

Heartstrings of the Earth

In pots they dance and sway,
Whispering secrets of the day.
With leaves like tiny green hats,
They cheer up the zany cats.

Their roots are tangled tales spun,
In the sun, they have so much fun.
Chasing dust bunnies with glee,
A leafy party for you and me.

If you spill a drop or two,
They shrug and say, "Just a dew!"
With laughter that fills the room,
They bloom and chase away the gloom.

So here's to pets of the floor,
From the window ledge to the door.
A quirky bunch, they thrive and swirl,
Life's nature's funny little whirl.

Hiding in the Clusters

In little groups, they find a nook,
Reading jokes from a tiny book.
Swinging leaves, like a playful show,
They giggle at the world below.

A home for bugs that like to hide,
They're like a green brigade with pride.
With spritz of water, they cheer and leap,
A leafy party that never sleeps.

In corners bright, they sprawl with flair,
Their green confetti fills the air.
Here's one hiding in the shade,
While another plans a leaf parade.

So if you need a giggle quick,
Find them laughing, not being sick.
For these green buddies, full of fun,
Make every day feel like a pun!

Comfort in the Canopy

Up above the furniture's plight,
They wave their arms, a silly sight.
In the canopy, they make a nest,
Finding solace in their leafy fest.

With twists and turns, they play a game,
Each leaf's a player, none the same.
They chuckle when the cat strolls by,
"Too much fluff!" they seem to cry.

Unruly curls that flop and twist,
Like playful strands, they can't resist.
They hide from dust in green disguise,
While flipping off the morning sighs.

So hang them high, they're ready to cheer,
Bringing laughter when you're near.
In every nook, they bloom and prance,
With hilarious charm, they take a chance.

Petals of Peace

In a jungle of laughter, they bloom,
Wrapping the room in leafy costume.
With every twist, they shout, "Hooray!"
As they frolic throughout the day.

Each leaf a giggle, a soft embrace,
Floating in bright, happy space.
When worries creep, they wiggle and sway,
Dancing away the blues of the day.

So pause a moment, let them guide,
In leafy hugs, you can confide.
These playful greens with smiles to share,
Add humor and joy to the air.

Petals of peace, they know the score,
In their company, you'll never bore.
With every glance, don't look too flat,
For nature's punchline is where it's at!

Nestled in Nature

In a pot so round, they sway,
Green warriors in bright display.
With leaves that dance and curl with glee,
Who knew they'd bring such joy to me?

They stretch their arms, they say hello,
To passing cats who stop and stow.
If only plants could tell a joke,
Their laughter bursts, a leafy cloak.

A dash of sun, a sprinkle of rain,
They sip their drink, then sip again.
As I pretend to take a cue,
The leaves just shrug, "What's wrong with you?"

So here they sit, with memes to share,
In verdant hues, without a care.
A bunch of greens with hearts so light,
They'll plot a prank in sheer delight.

The Poetry of Green

With tendrils reaching to the floor,
They weave a tale, just look—what's more!
These green companions never tire,
Their leaves ignite a lush desire.

As sunlight spills, the shadows play,
I swear they wink and sneak away.
A silly troop with endless charms,
They throw a dance in tiny balms.

I often chat to them at noon,
They nod along to every tune.
If I could trade my worries here,
Their laughter grows—the end is near!

So here's my ode, with giggles bright,
To leafy friends who hug me tight.
In moments shared of joy so keen,
They make my world a poem green.

Foliage and Reflection

In cozy nooks, they drum and thrum,
Their melodies, a gentle hum.
These leafy pals, misunderstood,
Bring giggles forth, yes, they're quite good!

With leaves adorned in shades so bright,
They whisper secrets in the night.
If one should droop, they all conspire,
To cheer up friends, they never tire.

A little spritz, a hearty laugh,
They share their joy on every path.
If only folks would see their quirk,
They'd shine so bright, let worries lurk!

So raise your cup and toast with cheer,
To leafy souls, let's draw them near.
In every twist and every bend,
These plants remind us, life's a friend.

Hushed Conversations

In corners quiet, pot friends meet,
With whispers soft, they share a treat.
They gossip 'bout the bugs they spy,
While I just sip my tea nearby.

They chatter 'bout the sun's warm kiss,
And bathe in joy, a leafy bliss.
"Oh look, a cat! Quick, hide your leaves!"
Their playful ways, the heart believes.

If silence falls, they mumble low,
In leafy language, fast they flow.
As I pretend to know their lingo,
They plot a scheme, a little bingo.

So here they sit, whimsical crew,
A motley band of green déjà vu.
Through all their schemes and silly plights,
They bring me laughter, day and nights.

Sanctuary of Green Hues

In a pot so bright, they dance with glee,
Little green wanderers, wild and free.
They twist and tangle, like hair in a mess,
Claiming all corners, they're here to impress.

With light-hearted whispers, they play hide and seek,
Sipping on sunshine, but oh, how they squeak!
When dust bunnies come, they throw a big fit,
"Hey, call the cat! We won't budge an inch!"

Their leaves wave hello like a friendly brigade,
Creating a haven where laughter won't fade.
In a world full of chaos, they're making a stand,
Green little jesters, with humor so grand.

Amidst all the petals, they frolic and jest,
Sprouting new tangents, they never find rest.
So here's to the greens, with a wink and a grin,
In their leafy domain, let the fun begin!

Tapestry of Tranquility

In a corner of calm, they giggle and sway,
Crafting their world in a mischievous way.
Their long, wavy leaves are a green comedy,
With every new sprout, it's a leafy jubilee.

They whisper sweet secrets, those leafy comedians,
Plotting a party with unseen medians.
With a flick of a leaf, they tickle your mind,
"Join our green shindig, we're one of a kind!"

When watering time comes, the show's really on,
They bobble and wobble, acting like a con.
With each little droplet, they shimmy and sway,
"Just call us the stars of the verdant ballet!"

Beneath the broad sun, their laughter takes flight,
In a lush, leafy haven, everything feels right.
No worries in sight, only giggles and cheer,
In our tapestry green, the joy is sincere!

Lush Leafy Soliloquies

In the warmth of the room, they plot a parade,
Whispering nonsense in leafy charade.
"Care for a dance? Come on, don't be shy!
We float like the breeze, let's reach for the sky!"

Their chatter is pleasant, a soft, rustling tone,
Reminding you gently, you're never alone.
With tiny green hands, they wave out their cheer,
"Join us in laughter, we start right here!"

Potting mix parties, with snacks made of sun,
They boast of their roots, claiming victory's fun.
"Leafy Olympics, our sport is quite rare,
We climb to new heights, without any care!"

So here in this space, with joy all around,
Embrace the green giggles; let laughter be found.
In their playful domain, mischief is key,
For in leafy soliloquies, we're wild and free!

Driftwood and Foliage

On driftwood they lounge, so cheeky and spry,
Sipping on sunlight, they reach for the sky.
In this forest of fun, they make quite a scene,
With leaves like confetti, they bounce and they preen.

"Let's throw a soirée!" they cheer with delight,
Each leaf holds an invite, it's simply a sight.
A shindig with roots, and laughter galore,
Where antics ensue, oh, who could want more?

They tumble and jiggle, their laughter's a blast,
Poking and prodding, they're having a cast.
And every new sprout is a welcome surprise,
In their driftwood domain, let the fun rise!

So here's to the green, the jesters of time,
Their charismatic charm, a playful chime.
With driftwood as throne, and the sun as their guide,
In this mad little garden, joy won't subside!

Comfort Found in the Living Veil

In corners green, they dangle low,
The tangled twists, a leafy show.
They sway and jiggle with such glee,
Plant-parent pondering: how to be free?

Each leaf a prankster, no doubt about,
Whispering secrets, causing a rout.
A hairdryer's wind, a mealtime feast,
In their leafy kingdom, I'm but a beast.

With every droop, an invitation to play,
I laugh at their antics, they brighten my day.
Who needs a pet when leaves can tease?
In their leafy laughter, I find my ease.

So here they thrive, a humorous crowd,
Making my space lively, cheerful, and loud.
In their viney expanse, I dance and I spin,
Comfort I find where the fun begins!

Nature's Breath in Indoor Corners

Green fingers wave in the morning light,
They sway to the rhythm, so sprightly, so bright.
A gentle breeze tickles their tips,
As I sip my coffee, they throw little quips.

Each droplet of water, a sparkling joke,
"I'm thirsty!" they whisper, with leaves that provoke.
A wink and a nod from a frond up high,
I chuckle out loud as I pass them by.

In pots made of clay, with soil so rich,
They beg for attention, a playful little hitch.
"Oh, feed me more nutrients, human, you know!"
With humor and plants, my worries let go.

Amidst the room's dullness, they light up the air,
The lush greenery—my source of repair.
So here's to the jesters that grow indoors,
Breathing in laughter, they open new doors.

The Sigh of Leaves in Quiet Moments

In a sunbeam's glow, they stretch and sway,
Whispering softly, they dance in the play.
"Look at us shine!" one leaf proclaims,
Another retorts, "We're not here for fame!"

They listen intently, my daily woes,
With every sigh, a gentle propose.
"Let's laugh at the world, it's all a charade,
While I droop a bit, no need to be afraid!"

I talk to the leaves; they nod back in glee,
With wisdom so vast, I feel so carefree.
Here in our haven of vibrant cheer,
They cradle my spirit, my laughter sincere.

In silence, they giggle, in rustles, they tease,
Creating a symphony that puts me at ease.
The sighing leaves make every moment bright,
I find my solace in their comic delight.

Verdant Whispers in Stillness

When all is quiet, they murmur away,
With leafy gossip, they start to play.
"Did you hear the news from the cactus next door?"
"What's spiky and grumpy? That plant, we implore!"

In patches of sunlight, they gather and chat,
"Let's plot a takeover, imagine that!"
A daring adventure in pots of delight,
As they scheme and they dream of a garden at night.

I snicker and snort at their playful plight,
How can such green bring absurdities to light?
Dancing their dance, spinning their yarn,
In their leafy humor, I'm blissfully charmed.

With verdant whispers echoing the room,
They bring a tickle, dispelling all gloom.
A laughter so bright, it blooms in my soul,
In their leafy embrace, I feel truly whole.

A Cocoon of Green Beneath the Window

In the sun by the curtain, oh what a sight,
Green tendrils dance gently, a curious delight.
They stretch out their arms as if waving hello,
Inviting the world to join in on the show.

With a touch of rebellion, they hang with such flair,
Complaining of water, but who really cares?
They're sassy and bold, with roots of pure glee,
These leafy companions are all about free!

The cat finds their beauty far too hard to resist,
And pounces with glee, with a flick of the wrist.
But the plants only chuckle, in tones of green cheer,
"Try as you might, we're rooted right here!"

So here in this nook, where sunshine does spill,
Laughter and foliage create quite the thrill.
With a splash of the silly, and a whole lot of fun,
In this cocoon of delight, every day's a new run.

Gentle Stirrings of Life and Peace.

In the corner, they nestle, where stillness aligns,
With a twitch and a wiggle, they dance out the lines.
These green friends speak softly in whispers of cheer,
Sharing secrets of wellness, for all who draw near.

Each leaf has a story, a giggle, a grin,
They tickle the air with a light-hearted spin.
They sway to the rhythm of life's gentle song,
In a world full of haste, they simply belong.

"Water me more!" they chant, in a playful jest,
A chorus of leaves, wanting only the best.
But when the sun peeks, they bask in the glow,
With smiles made of chlorophyll, ready to grow!

So here in this haven, where giggles are found,
Nature's own jesters are playfully bound.
A beautiful mess of green joy on display,
In gentle stirrings, life dances away.

Green Whispers in Quiet Corners

In a quiet nook, where shadows do meet,
Green whispers giggle, oh, what a treat!
They huddle together, sharing a joke,
Life's little secrets in every soft poke.

With tips on hydration, they lean to advise,
"Just a little more water, and we'll surely rise!"
But it's all in good fun, just playful banter,
These leafy comedians, full of good laughter!

A fluttering breeze makes their laughter cascade,
As tiny leaves rustle in whimsical charade.
They gossip in shades of emerald delight,
Painting the corners with joy, day or night.

So come have a chuckle by this leafy delight,
In their green-hued realm, everything feels right.
With a splash of good humor, they weave just the best,
In these quiet corners, we all find our rest.

Tendrils of Peace

Oh, the tendrils twist gracefully, seeking their fate,
In a world full of chaos, they flutter and wait.
With a wink and a nudge, they curl here and there,
Transforming our spaces with style and with flair.

They call out "No worries, just follow your bliss!"
With leaves that are laughing, how could you miss?
Each playful green twist, a sign of a cheer,
They sprinkle the air with a light-hearted jeer.

When friends drop on by, they stop and they stare,
At these little green creatures with an easy care.
"Where have you been hiding?" they jovially ask,
These entertainers thrive in a lush leafy mask!

So join in the fun, let your worries all cease,
Among these soft tendrils, you'll find your peace.
In the happiness blooming from every green thread,
A tapestry woven, where laughter is spread.

Resting Under the Leaves

In a pot so snug and round,
Leaves overhead, what a crown!
Chatting with the sunlit beams,
Sipping on my leafy dreams.

A cat thinks it's a jungle scene,
Chasing shadows, living clean.
I laugh as he takes a dive,
Into the greens where hopes arrive.

The dust bunnies join the play,
Organizing a fun ballet.
With every wiggle, every twirl,
It's quite the dance in my leafy world!

So here I sit, a funky host,
Enjoying nature's playful boast.
In my oasis, wild and free,
Living life, just leaf and me!

Embers of a Gentle Spirit

Curled up in the morning light,
I brew some tea, oh, what a sight!
The leaves beside me dance in glee,
Like they're sharing a cup with me!

A tiny bug takes a bold leap,
And stirs the calm, oh, what a creep!
But I just chuckle, sip my brew,
Nature's circus, all in view!

With every petal, every stalk,
My worries fade, no need to talk.
Breathe in deep, let laughter ring,
In this space where hearts take wing.

We share the silence, me and green,
Where joy and chaos meet unseen.
In leafy patches, life's a game,
Funny how I'm never the same!

In the Heart of Green

In the center of my little zone,
Leaves laugh softly, all alone.
A quirky plant with snaky grace,
Brought a smile to my dreary face.

Beneath the fronds, I hear a song,
A tune where I feel I belong.
Each leaf whispers funnier things,
Like tales of mice wearing tiny rings.

A neighbor's dog comes prancing by,
To sniff the pots and say hi.
But little does he understand,
These leaves are more than just a stand!

With every sunbeam, joy ignites,
We gather 'round for daily rites.
In leafy laughter, peace extends,
With every glance, humor wends!

Cultivating Calm

With a sprinkle and a sigh, oh dear,
I question why I'm even here.
Yet the green leaves wave, so spry,
    Reminding me to give a try.

Wild thoughts dance in leafy shades,
They're like flash mobs in the glades!
Every time I pause and stare,
I giggle, what a cute affair!

The sunlight steals the spotlight near,
As the plants toss laughter, oh so clear.
I'm flung into this vibrant chase,
Chasing joy in this green embrace.

So here I sit, my heart is light,
In this patch of green delight.
Cultivating calm with every sprout,
With a chuckle, I'm all about!

Where Light Meets Green

In corners bright, they twirl and sway,
My leafy friends, they dance all day.
With tendrils long, they twist and bend,
Their playful charm, a leafy trend.

They drink the sun, they sip the air,
Don't mind the dust, it's part of their flair.
With pots that boast, a verdant scene,
They plot and scheme like a garden queen.

Each morning fresh, they greet the dawn,
With little leaves, they'll carry on.
They cradle hearts with every gleam,
A comic act, a leafy dream.

So here's to greens, they brighten lives,
In their green realm, good humor thrives.
With wiggles, giggles, so full of glee,
My leafy pals, just let them be!

Echoes of the Foliage

They whisper secrets in the room,
With fronds that wave, they cast out gloom.
In pots diverse, they hold a joke,
A leafy laugh, a banter spoke.

In crafty vines, they play charades,
With leafy pranks, they make parades.
Like little sprites, they leap and hop,
No end to fun, they never stop.

They toss their leaves like confetti bright,
A wild party in morning light.
With every twist, their joy expands,
In a dance-off, they take a stand.

A jungle jest, they can't be tamed,
In their green world, nothing's claimed.
They're comic trees, forever keen,
For laughter found in shades of green!

A Lullaby of Green

In quiet rooms, they sing a song,
Of gentle greens that hum along.
Their leafy voices, soft and sweet,
A melody that can't be beat.

With every sway, they strum a line,
A tune of peace, both bright and fine.
They wiggle roots, a tender rhyme,
In blooming time, they steal the prime.

When night approaches, they hush their cheer,
With soothing tones, they draw me near.
A lullaby of greens so deep,
In leafy dreams, I fall asleep.

So here's to flora, bold and bright,
In leafy realms, a pure delight.
With nature's song, they wrap me tight,
In charming arms 'til morning light.

Caress of the Climbing

They scale the shelves with playful might,
Those cheeky vines, a wondrous sight.
They stretch so tall, like little climbers,
In search of sun, like tiny timers.

A twist here, turn there, a lovely game,
They reach for dreams, they chase the flame.
With tendrils bright, they grasp and play,
In leafy fun, they steal the day.

With every inch, they claim their throne,
The rulers of my humble home.
Their laughter echoes in the light,
A frolicsome dance, such sheer delight.

So let them climb, let them explore,
For in their growth, I can't ignore.
With coaxing cheer, they always thrive,
In every leaf, their joys arrive!

Moments Among the Leaves

In a pot they dance and sway,
Chasing dust bunnies all day.
Hanging like performers on high,
Who'd have thought plants could fly?

With each twist, they tease the air,
Naughty little green affair.
A leaf fell down right on my nose,
Oh, the giggles that it chose!

When they stretch, they touch the sky,
Never shy, oh my, oh my!
Not just foliage, but a crew,
Making mischief, just for you!

In the morning light they glow,
Whispering secrets only they know.
They plot to grow and take the space,
A leafy parade, oh what a race!

Ripples of Green

In the corner, they start to sway,
Testing out their leafy ballet.
A gentle breeze makes them giggle,
With a little twist and a wiggle.

Their roots are deep, their hearts are fun,
Playing hide-and-seek 'til the day is done.
If they could speak, oh what a show,
Tales of mischief only they know!

They drop their leaves like confetti fair,
Surprising me with gentle flair.
I sweep them up, their laugh in tow,
How these plants manage to steal the show!

In pots they gather, a leafy crew,
Dreams of adventure, they pursue.
Who knew greenery could throw a bash?
Every plant party ends with a splash!

Shadows and Serenity

In the shade, they twist and pout,
Playing games, there's never doubt.
Who needs sunlight? Not this lot!
In the corner, they plot a plot.

Chatting softly, leaf to leaf,
Gossiping about my disbelief.
They joke about a spider's web,
How it made me shriek and ebb!

Each dangling limb, a prankster's dream,
Creating chaos, or so it seems.
A gentle tug, a playful tease,
I'm their audience, they aim to please!

With playful hops, they sway so free,
Crafting laughter, just you and me.
In this green embrace, we find delight,
Together we shine, from day to night!

Breaths of Nature

In my home, they take a stand,
Giggling plants, oh so grand!
With every breath, they share their cheer,
A leafy party, always near!

Chatting roots beneath the ground,
With whispers soft, the joy is found.
They wink at me, the silly sights,
Hooting like they're up all night!

Every leaf, a quirky grin,
In this green world, let's begin.
Sipping sunlight, feeling bold,
Stories of laughter to be told!

They sway and swing in playful dance,
Living life like it's their chance.
With a chuckle and a giggle spree,
Nature's laughter, wild and free!

The Calm Within Reach

In my little corner of green,
Leaves dancing as if to preen.
A jungle thriving, oh what a sight,
Who knew plants could bring such delight?

Water the roots, and watch them sway,
Happiness grows in a quirky way.
A little sun, a splash of glee,
These leafy buddies bring joy to me.

They don't cry or make a fuss,
Just sit quiet, no need to rush.
In this house of emerald cheer,
I find my peace, oh dear, oh dear!

So here's to greens, both bright and bold,
A story of joy quietly told.
Just add some light, and oh my friend,
You'll find laughter around each bend.

Espressivo in Green

A pot of joy, so plump and bright,
With leaves that dance in morning light.
I sip my coffee, smile and say,
My green friends really steal the day!

One leaf is small, another so wide,
In this little arena, they all preside.
They wave goodbye as I leave the room,
Competing to spread their leafy bloom!

I tell them secrets, they nod along,
Each little whisper feels like a song.
Oh, how I giggle, they've got such flair,
Green conspirators in my cozy lair!

So here's to mornings with coffee and greens,
A symphony of laughter amidst the scenes.
With each little sprout, I find my groove,
Trust me, these leaves have all the moves!

Leaves Telling Stories

Once was a leaf that climbed so high,
In search of stories beneath the sky.
It met a shadow, tall and wide,
And whispered secrets, never to hide.

One told of days when sunshine spilled,
While others rumbled as raindrops thrilled.
They giggled and rustled, sharing their tales,
In this leafy realm where laughter prevails.

They plotted adventures in pots of clay,
Imagining travels far away.
And I, the audience, chuckled along,
With every twist, they prove me wrong!

So plant a little joy, watch it thrive,
Let every leaf help your spirits survive.
For in their whispers, I always find,
Life's a good story, entwined and entwined.

Nature's Resting Place

In a world where worries bloom,
I found a corner free of gloom.
With green companions, I take my seat,
A sanctuary where joys repeat.

The leaves chatter as I unwind,
In their calm, a laugh I find.
No rush, no hurry, just peace of mind,
A home for hearts and leaves intertwined.

They stretch and relax, as I sigh deep,
Witnessing moments I choose to keep.
An oasis of fun in every sway,
Nature's humor brightens my day!

So let's toast to greens, both quirky and fun,
Here's to laughter beneath the sun.
In this resting place, my soul's set free,
With my leafy friends, forever we'll be!

Nature's Embrace in Urban Spaces

In a pot on the sill, they dance with glee,
Waving their arms like they're wild and free.
Spying on pigeons with a cheeky grin,
Nature's rebels, where chaos begins.

While office folk toil, they take a break,
Basking in sunlight, the joy they make.
Little green warriors, they stand so proud,
In a world of gray, they're nature's crowd.

Hoisting a leaf, like a flag on high,
Encouraging smiles, as by they pass by.
Replacing the stress with a gentle cheer,
Who knew green could be the best career?

In a jungle of concrete, they sneak about,
Spreading their laughter, no reason to pout.
With roots in the soil, they secretly thrive,
Tickling our hearts, they keep dreams alive.

Green Breath in Concrete Cages

Amidst the asphalt, they wiggle and sway,
Telling the sun, 'Come on, let's play!'
With tendrils of joy, they conquer the gloom,
Sprucing up spaces that once felt like doom.

They share whispered secrets, a leafy affair,
Eavesdropping on gossip, no need to care.
With spindly fingers, they weave through the air,
Charming the neighbors, a botanical dare.

When raindrops arrive, they throw a parade,
Slurping the droplets like lemonade made.
They bounce in the wind, each petal a shout,
Who knew plants could have fun, beyond any doubt?

Hidden in corners, their laughter resounds,
Turning dull moments to playful rounds.
In cages of concrete, they laugh and they sing,
Oh, the joy that these green comrades can bring!

Serenity Woven in Chlorophyll Hues

Bright green shades weave a tapestry grand,
A riot of chaos in a tiny pot stand.
With bobbing green leaves, they've got charm for days,
Turning mundane hours into joyful plays.

While city lights twinkle, they quietly plot,
To find ways to brighten up every hot spot.
A tease here and there, a playful surprise,
As they reach for a window, competing with skies.

With friends all around in a cozy green nook,
They host the best parties, no need for a book.
With petals and laughter, what more can one need?
In this happy jungle, they plant joy with speed!

Tickling the air as they sway in delight,
They dance through the evenings, a glorious sight.
With visions of comfort, they conquer the hue,
Who knew such calm could come colored so true?

Velvet Leaves and Soft Shadows

Oh, velvet leaves with a hit of sass,
Playing hide and seek for a laugh in a glass.
They lounge on the sill, plotting their schemes,
Whispering stories to the bright morning beams.

Those soft shadows play on the walls so bright,
Giving a wink to the night's gentle light.
In their leafy retreat, the giggles unfold,
As they battle the dust; oh, the tales must be told!

They flourish in quiet, in chaos abound,
Turning dull mornings to a merry-go-round.
So if you feel heavy, come join in the fun,
With these leafy pals, you'll never be done!

Velvet leaves laughing, a verdant surprise,
Catching the daydreams like butterflies.
Tiny green jesters, each leaf on display,
In their cozy kingdom, all worries decay.

Embracing Life in Shadows

In corners they lounge, green and spry,
Stretching their limbs, reaching for the sky.
Chasing the sun, plotting their scheme,
While laughing at all that we humans deem.

With leaves like confetti, they dance with glee,
"Water us more!" they shout in esprit.
Climbing up shelves, they take over the space,
Debating the cat, who's lost in their grace.

They weave through the chaos, a soft little cheer,
Turning the mundane to something sincere.
A vacuum of joy in a tiny green form,
Reminding us all that it's fine to perform.

So here's to the greens, who never complain,
Making our lives feel less like a strain.
With a wink and a nod, they keep us inspired,
In the shadows of comfort, always desired.

Threads of Rejuvenation

Oh, little green beings, you know how to thrive,
Weaving your magic, making us feel alive.
With quirky little tendrils that dangle and sway,
You'd think we'd planted a comedian today!

In pots by the window, they shimmer and shine,
Practicing yoga, oh how they entwine.
Dropping their leaves like a party confetti,
While we stand amused, feeling all warm and petty.

When life gets too busy, with a scream and a shout,
Those leafy companions know what it's about.
Perched on the desk, with a grin on their face,
They remind us to slow down, find our own pace.

With each little sprout, we giggle and cheer,
Transforming our living space into a sphere.
Of laughter and light, where worries collide,
In a world that's so hectic, they're a joy to abide.

A Breath of Green

In the stillness of morning, they silent resound,
A quirky little whisper, a soft leafy sound.
"Wake up, sleepyhead, it's time to unroll!"
They beam with a vibe that can brighten your soul.

With jokes in their leaves, and puns in their roots,
Our little green friends are wearing their boots.
They shimmy and shake, in the soft morning light,
As if they are saying, "Come dance, feel the delight!"

How they cheerfully flourish, it's truly a show,
Plant antics so funny, who knew they would glow?
In their leafy embrace, all worries grow small,
Who thought a bit of green could answer the call?

So here's to the jesters, with chlorophyll flair,
Turning our frowns into giggles and care.
As we breathe in the joy that their presence imparts,
We find that their laughter goes straight to our hearts.

The Calm Inside

Within tender leaves lies a laugh-filled trance,
They sway with the rhythm, they know how to dance.
In a pot on the sill, they keep company fine,
With a chuckle or two, or a mischievous line.

When chaos erupts in this bustling old place,
The greenery smiles with tranquility's grace.
"Just chill!" they proclaim, with a wild leafy cheer,
As we pour out our woes, they lend us their ear.

Furry little neighbors, they never judge harsh,
As they coax us to breathe, rolling out the parched.
Each droplet of water a drip of pure glee,
Nourishing laughter, nurturing simplicity.

So here's to their wisdom, the green therapy crew,
As we find solace in their vibrant debut.
Through tangled adventures, their joy is sincere,
A calm and sweet laughter—a true atmosphere!

www.ingramcontent.com/pod-product-compliance
Lightning Source LLC
Chambersburg PA
CBHW072120070526
44585CB00016B/1514